Contents

How stressed are you?

Answer the following questions and work out your 'stress profile'. To what extent do you suffer from stress? How can you best focus your stress relief efforts?

How many of the following symptoms do you have: irritability; difficulty concentrating; feeling 'put upon'; loss of sense of humour; constant tiredness; loss of appetite; insomnia; nail biting; indigestion; food cravings; nausea?

a) 1–4   b) 5–8   c) 9–11

How many of the following hassles do you experience: lots of travelling; long hours; client/customer troubles; difficult office politics; tight deadlines; cumbersome bureaucracy; making mistakes; work interfering with personal life; too many dull tasks; worries about job security; constant interruptions?

a) 1–4   b) 5–8   c) 9–11

How do you feel about the amount of information that comes your way every week?

a) No problems. Anything unnecessary is immediately filed – in the bin!
b) OK. I have a clearout every so often, otherwise it all gets too much.
c) Overwhelmed – there is no way I can take it all in.

Deal with stress

How to improve the way you work

A & C Black • London

Revised edition first published in Great Britain 2010

A & C Black Publishers Ltd
36 Soho Square
London W1D 3QY
www.acblack.com

Copyright © A & C Black Publishers Ltd, 2010

First edition 2004 © Bloomsbury Publishing, 2004
Reprinted 2006, 2007 by A & C Black Publishers Ltd

A CIP record for this book is available from the British Library.

ISBN: 978–14081–2808–4

This book is produced using paper that is made from wood grown in
managed, sustainable forests. It is natural, renewable and
recyclable. The logging and manufacturing processes conform to
the environmental regulations of the country of origin.

Design by Fiona Pike, Pike Design, Winchester
Typeset by RefineCatch Limited, Bungay, Suffolk
Printed in Spain by GraphyCems

How do you react to unexpected difficulties?
a) I think about ways of dealing with the problem from its source outwards.
b) I try to follow solutions to similar problems in the past.
c) I'm not a great problem solver and so I panic.

How would you describe the process of delegation?
a) It's an important process for the development of yourself and your staff.
b) It's a useful tool – if you haven't got time to do something, pass it on!
c) I see it as laziness. If a job comes your way, it is up to you to deal with it.

How many of the following do you experience regularly: feeling ignored; difficulty expressing opinions; feeling 'put upon'; sense of inferiority; extreme gratefulness when your opinion is sought; sense of being out of control of meetings; trouble saying 'no'?
a) 1–2   b) 3–4   c) 5–7

How would you describe the management culture in your organisation?
a) Generally open and friendly.
b) Managers can be intimidating at times.
c) Employees often feel 'steamrollered', even bullied.

How do you view the level of morale in your organisation?
a) Pretty high – there is an air of satisfaction and achievement.
b) There are always malcontents, but it's generally fine.
c) Very low. Several colleagues are thinking of leaving.

a = 1, b = 2, and c = 3.

Now add up your scores.

Chapter **1** is useful to everyone as it will help you identify the forms stress can take, and give you advice on how to get your stress levels back under control.

- **18–24:** You are probably near the end of your tether – but help is at hand! Read Chapters **8** and **6** if the problem lies with difficult work colleagues or communication breakdowns. If you can work more effectively as a team, this will allow you more time to take control of your workload (Chapters **2**, **3**, and **5**). Chapter **7** offers advice for managers on improving morale, and if your stress is caused by hitting your head against brick wall when trying to solve problems, Chapter **4** suggests new ways round them.

- **12–17:** You suffer from moderate levels of stress. Conduct a 'time audit' and follow the advice given in Chapters **2** and **3** to improve your work–life balance. Support this with advice in Chapter **6** on how to assert yourself if feeling downtrodden, and learn the value of effective delegation from Chapter **5**.

- **8–11:** Stress hasn't got the better of you – *yet*! Conduct a 'time audit' (Chapter **2**) as a preventative measure. This will make you more aware of your work–life balance and help you identify possible sources of stress in the future.

Dealing with stress
by Cary Cooper and Susan Cartwright
lecturers in organisational psychology and health

For many individuals, joining the enterprise culture has entailed a substantial personal cost: stress. The word 'stress' has found as firm a place in our modern lexicon as 'fast food', 'mobiles' and 'CDs'. 'It's a high stress job', people often say, awarding an odd sort of prestige to an occupation.

But for people whose ability to cope with day-to-day matters is at crisis point, the concept of stress is not a matter of bravado. For them, stress can be translated as *pain*.

Step one: Spot the symptoms

It's important to be able to distinguish between pressure and stress. Pressure is motivating, stimulating, and energising. But when pressure exceeds our ability to cope, stress is produced. Continued high levels of stress can, at worst, result in illness, depression or even nervous breakdown. However, there are a number of signals that help you detect when your levels of stress are bordering on dangerous.

✔ Take a good look at your well-being. If you experience any number of the following behavioural and physical symptoms on a frequent or near-constant basis, it might be time to start looking for causes and to reassess your priorities. These symptoms may be your body's way of telling you that you have crossed over the dividing line between healthy pressure and harmful stress.

Behavioural symptoms

- Constant irritability with people
- Difficulty in making decisions
- Loss of sense of humour
- Suppressed anger
- Difficulty concentrating
- Inability to finish one task before rushing into another
- Feeling the target of other people's animosity
- Feeling unable to cope
- Wanting to cry at the smallest problem
- Lack of interest in doing things after returning home from work
- Waking up in the morning and feeling tired after an early night
- Constant tiredness

Physical symptoms

- Lack of appetite
- Craving for food when under pressure
- Frequent indigestion or heartburn
- Constipation or diarrhoea
- Insomnia
- Tendency to sweat for no good reason
- Nervous twitches or nail biting
- Headaches
- Cramps and muscle spasms
- Nausea
- Breathlessness without exertion
- Fainting spells
- Impotency or frigidity
- Eczema

Step two: Identify the sources of stress at work

Once you've admitted that you're not coping with the everyday pressures of work, the next step in the process is to identify the source(s) of the stress in the workplace. Once this is done, you can draw up a plan of action to minimise or eliminate the excess pressure or damaging source of stress.

✔ Make a note of problem areas. The table below identifies some possible daily hassles that trouble people at work. There are, of course, more significant problem areas as well, such as coping with redundancy, dealing with a bullying boss or trying to cope with a dysfunctional corporate culture (one that demands excessive working hours or employs an autocratic management style).

Daily hassles at work

- Trouble with client/customer
- Having to work late
- Constant interruptions
- Trouble with boss
- Deadlines and time pressures
- Decision-making
- Dealing with the bureaucracy at work
- Travelling associated with the job
- Making mistakes
- Conflict with organisational goals
- Job interfering with home/family life
- Can't cope with in-tray
- Can't say 'no' to work
- Not enough stimulating things to do

- Technological breakdowns
- Trouble with work colleagues
- Tasks associated with job not stimulating
- Too much responsibility
- Too many jobs to do at once
- Telephone interruptions
- Travelling to and from work
- Too many meetings

- Don't know where career going
- Worried about job security
- Spouse/partner not supportive about work
- Family life adversely affecting work
- Having to tell subordinates unpleasant things, e.g. redundancy

Step three: Manage the daily hassles

I Manage time

Of all the daily hassles experienced by managers, one of the most stressful is poor time management. Time wasters fall into four categories, requiring different solutions.

- **The mañanas.** People who fall into this category cause themselves problems because they procrastinate, preferring to 'think' about work rather than 'do' it. Procrastination often stems from boredom, a lack of confidence or reluctance to seek clarification.

TOP TIPS FOR MAÑANAS

✔ Break up overwhelming tasks into smaller jobs.

> ✔ Draw up a 'to do' list of all the tasks you need to complete in the short term (that is, within the next week) and in the long term.
>
> ✔ When planning your work schedule, attempt to balance routine tasks with the more enjoyable jobs.
>
> ✔ Accept that risks are inevitable and that no decisions are ever made on the basis of complete information.

- **The poor delegators.** People who fall into this category waste a considerable amount of their time doing work that could easily and more effectively have been done by somebody else.

> **TOP TIPS FOR POOR DELEGATORS**
>
> ✔ Delegation does not mean abdication.
>
> ✔ Always take time out to explain exactly what is required; poor delegators are often also poor communicators, which is why they are frequently disappointed with the efforts of others.
>
> ✔ Having delegated a job, leave the person to get on with it.
>
> ✔ Avoid taking on unnecessary work by learning to say 'no' politely and assertively.

- **The disorganised.** People who fall into this category are instantly recognisable by the mounds of paper that form barricades around their desks. Disorganised individuals frequently miss or are late for appointments. These people frequently think their problems are due to work overload rather than their own poor organisational skills.

TOP TIPS FOR THE DISORGANISED
✔ Plan effectively before taking action.
✔ Make a 'to do' list regularly at the start of each day and review it each evening.
✔ Stick to one task and finish it!
✔ Think before you telephone; draw up a list of all the information you require from the caller.
✔ Reserve your prime time, when your energy levels are high, for complex tasks, and save the trivial routine tasks for non-prime time.
✔ When making an appointment in your diary, enter a finish time as well as a start time.

■ **The mushrooms.** People who fall into this category are usually unclear about the purpose and objectives of what they are required to do. They constantly speculate and inwardly question what they should do rather than do it. They lack assertiveness and communication skills.

TOP TIPS FOR MUSHROOMS
✔ Learn to say 'I don't know', when you don't know something.

✔ **Learn to say 'I don't understand' when you don't understand a task, a role, or objective.**

2 Manage interruptions

Another source of personal stress at work for many managers is 'constant interruptions', from the telephone, e-mail or drop-by colleagues.

■ **New technology.** In terms of voice mail, e-mail, mobile phones and the like, it is important to manage the technology rather than let the technology manage you.

TOP TIPS FOR MANAGING TECHNOLOGY

✔ **For telephone calls:** batch your phone calls; plan what you are going to say and need to know in advance and deliberately discipline yourself by placing specific time limits on the length of a call.

✔ **For voice mail:** only use this when you need space to carry out complex tasks requiring your full attention, and don't be tempted to access your voice mail messages every ten minutes! Also deal with those messages that are most important first; deal with the others later.

✔ **For e-mails:** prioritise your e-mails according to their importance to your objectives, then reply to them in this order. All too often, individuals reply to e-mails in order

> of their arrival and not in terms of their
> importance.
> ✔ **For mobiles:** don't keep your phone
> switched on all the time because it could
> interrupt an important meeting or activity.
> Use mobiles on journeys or during other
> periods of downtime to deal with work in your
> in-tray that you would otherwise have to deal
> with when back at work.

■ **Drop-by colleagues.** Although being interrupted can provide a welcome diversionary break from a boring or tedious task, too many interruptions during the course of the day are a waste of time, distracting and frequently irritating.

Interruptions occur for a number of reasons. The person involved may:

■ want to exchange information;
■ need reassurance or clarification;
■ lack confidence about a task;
■ want a casual chat because they need a break or are bored.

It is important to differentiate these reasons. If a colleague needs your input to do their job properly, you may need to spend some of your time with them. If not, there are a range of friendly but firm ways of curtailing or avoiding unnecessary interruptions from colleagues. Here are some suggestions to help you fend off unwanted visitors.

TOP TIPS FOR MANAGING DROP-BY COLLEAGUES

✔ Establish quiet hours during which you can work undisturbed. This may mean closing your door and putting a notice outside.

✔ Establish visiting hours when you are available for drop-in visitors.

✔ Arrange meetings away from your desk or office; this enables you to take control and leave when you want to.

✔ Do not hesitate to curb wafflers, in a polite and friendly manner, by asking them to make their main point(s).

✔ When unexpectedly interrupted, ask the person how much time he or she needs and, if you haven't got the space, then rearrange the meeting.

3 Accept the changing nature of work

One of the major sources of stress for managers today is the fact that jobs are no longer for life – job security is a thing of the past. Organisations expect employees to be more flexible, more accountable and to be hardworking and committed; at the same time, employers offer increasingly limited (or no) assurances or expectations of employment security and career development opportunities.

For significant numbers of future workers, the job is likely to become a freelance activity in the form of a series of temporarily or discretely defined tasks or projects undertaken either successively or concurrently for single or multiple employers.

For people currently working in 'delayered' organisational structures, coping with changed career expectations requires considerable personal adjustment: you need to accept that the onus for career management and training now rests with yourself rather than with the organisation. This requires a greater degree of initiative, personal planning and control.

Although the prospect of pursuing a self-determined career outside the structure of an established organisation might seem daunting, research evidence based on the experience of mid-life career changers suggests that increased job and life satisfaction is frequently gained from a move to freelancing and self-employment.

Step four: Plan to deal with your own stress

✔ Understand what causes *you* stress, when you are likely to become stressed and how you can avoid these situations. To help, it can be useful to think about previous times that were stressful for you and remember how you felt, how you reacted and behaved, what the result was and whether, with the benefit of hindsight, you handled it in the best way possible.

✔ Take responsibility. Too often, people either deny their problem, in which case it will almost certainly worsen, or blame someone (or something) else. Even if it is the fault of someone else, it is *you* that is being affected and *you* that needs to resolve it. People are often too afraid, ashamed or uncertain to admit that they are suffering from stress, but the longer they deny the problem, the worse the effects of the downward cycle.

✔ Consider what is causing stress. Is it resulting from the job, your role, work relationships, change or something else, perhaps not work-related at all? Knowing the symptoms and acknowledging the existence of stress is really only the start: the next key step is to identify the source of the stress. It can often be caused by an accumulation of factors piling on to each other. The solution is to rationally consider how to take down the wall that is encircling you, brick by brick. Stress is rarely removed in one clean sweep but often requires action in a range of areas.

✔ Anticipate stressful periods (either at work or home) and plan for them. This may include getting temporary resources or people with specific skills to help during a particular period.

✔ Develop strategies for handling stress. Consider what may have worked for you in the past, what you did and how successful it was. Also consider removing or reducing the cause of stress, or learning to accept it if it cannot be removed.

✔ Understand and use management techniques to prevent or reduce stress. For example, time management and assertiveness are two of the most important skills in reducing and handling stress, as many difficulties are caused either by time pressures or relationship issues that could be prevented by more assertive, controlled behaviour. Communication, decision-making and problem-solving also have much to offer once the problem has been acknowledged and the sources of stress are identified.

✔ Relax! This is easier said than done, but the key is to understand that you need to *work* at relaxing. This may mean planning a holiday or finding a hobby that suits you best and then *absorbing* yourself in it. At work too, try to take regular breaks away from your desk. A five minute stroll outside can revive worn-out eyes, brains, and nerves. Time away from the causes of stress can help to put the situation in perspective and lead to a new approach that provides a solution.

If you are responsible for preventing and reducing stress within organisations, you should:

✔ Acknowledge stress in others. As a leader, you should not be afraid to talk to someone if you think they are suffering from stress, and then be prepared to help and support them. Often, just acknowledging the existence of stress and showing understanding can provide enough energy to see the solution, remove the stress and ultimately overcome the problem.

✔ Build a positive team environment. It is possible to reduce stress for others by developing good communication systems, a supportive team approach, a blame-free environment and a clear sense of involvement and responsibility. Other factors that can also help include mentoring schemes that prevent, identify and treat cases of stress; appraisal systems and simply knowing and understanding the people that work with you. For some senior managers in large organisations, this may not be possible, in which case these values need to be passed down the chain of command so that they are supported throughout the organisation.

'In order that people may be happy in their work, these three things are needed: they must be fit for it; they must not do too much of it; and they must have a sense of success in it.'

John Ruskin, 1851

Common mistakes

✗ **You think you can do it all alone**
People sometimes take on too much, thinking that they can cope without additional support. Perhaps you think you are saving your organisation money by covering a number of responsibilities, but in reality you could be wasting money in missed opportunities or inefficiency. Often, under stress, the one thing we become incapable of doing well is delegating work appropriately. Better

communication and prioritising objectives are therefore essential. Identifying better resource management, prioritising the workload, building in contingency time, anticipating pressure points and monitoring progress are all important in dealing with stress.

✗ You don't say 'no'
Perhaps you're one of those people who are capable of sustaining high levels of activity over a long period of time, and it has become expected that you always perform at that pitch. Your colleagues are unlikely to be aware of the sacrifices being made. There may be no reward for your sacrifice – in fact, you may have additional work dumped on you. The solution is being assertive and saying 'no' when the pressure is too great.

✗ You succumb to a 'long hours culture' at work
In some organisations, stress creates status, where stress is interpreted as accomplishment. Many people put in long hours in the hope that their hard work will be noticed and rewarded, but are secretly resentful that they have to do this. Working on outputs rather than inputs will help define your success. Find out whether others view hard work as positive or not.

✗ You take it out on others
Stress is no respecter of boundaries. Stress from one aspect of your life will eventually affect all other elements of your life too. Try not to transfer the pressures to those who are not part of the problem. Work on the causes and not the symptoms.

STEPS TO SUCCESS

✔ Recognising the symptoms and understanding the causes of workplace stress is vital in preventing it becoming an issue.

✔ The changing nature of work makes stress more complex, varied and quite possibly more common. It is important to acknowledge that you are stressed and act upon that knowledge quickly – draw up a plan of action and follow it.

✔ Remember that you have to *work* at reducing stress – it won't happen by itself! The time you devote to managing stress will be repaid by increased efficiency and enjoyment of your time, both at work and at home.

Useful links

About.com-advice and resources on work-related topics:
http://stress.about.com
Mindtools.com-stress management techniques:
www.mindtools.com/smpage.html
Directgov:
www.direct.gov.uk/en/Employment/HealthAndSafety AtWork/DG_10026604

Organising your time

Time management is about making every moment effective by being truly focused and not dividing your energies by worrying about the past or future. However, it is still important to be able to keep the past, present and future in perspective. It is crucial to planning and prioritising. In this way you are able to set tasks in the right context. This gives a sense of order, structure, and security for those who are dependent upon your time management skills.

In our working lives, time is the one thing that is more and more in demand. There are so many tools for instant access to information and each other, the idea being that more time is released for increased efficiency and productivity. Although these tools are designed to save time, they can be so complex that they consume time and put additional pressures on managers.

Step one: Conduct a 'time audit'

It is useful to do a 'time audit' on your life. What is the balance between the demands that are placed upon you at work and the obligations and pleasures that define your private life? Does this balance satisfy you or do you find yourself sacrificing one activity for another? The key to good time management is being aware of the world in which you live and the interrelationships between the component parts and choosing how you apportion your time to each.

How to do it

1 Take a large sheet of paper and write your name at the centre.

2 Place around your name words that represent the demands upon your life. Include contracted work hours, travelling/commuting time, social hours at work – eating, post-work socialising – family commitments, remembering that your time demands are likely to increase depending on the number of children/ dependents that you have. Also include your wider family and friends, sporting or fitness activities, socialising time and time spent on hobbies or areas of personal interest.

3 Mark the number of hours that are dedicated to each of these areas throughout the day. You may want to use half hour intervals for clarity. This will graphically represent your life in terms of the choices and tradeoffs you are making in those areas that are important to you.

4 Ask yourself, 'Is this how I want to live my life?' You may sacrifice some important areas of your life in the short term, but be aware of what happens when a particular phase of your life comes to an end. How will you manage

this transition, particularly when it is an unexpected or sudden transition, such as a change in work circumstances or retirement?

5 Take a highlighting pen and mark those areas on your chart that need attention. If, for instance, you are spending too much time at work, you need to re-establish the objectives of your role and the demands placed upon you by others, and evaluate how you are going to get a better balance. Some of the time management toolkits outlined below will give you some ideas on how to do this.

Step two: Make adjustments

1 Be aware of your choices

The desire to be good at time management is half the battle but you need to be aware of the choices you have to make. These relate to your overall life balance and the values you hold.

✔ Look at what you are being asked to do and why. Is this because it is related to your role or because you hold a particular skill or expertise? Where you are being asked to do many things outside your area of responsibility, you may need to speak to your boss to clarify the boundaries of your responsibility.

There are always choices to be made. You may find that you can win more time by avoiding time spent on commuting and working from home. However, beware that your family don't automatically see this as additional capacity for them. You will need to create boundaries to ensure that your productivity remains high and that this new environment does not disrupt your efforts.

TOP TIP
Communicate with others where you have time conflicts and don't make commitments that you know you can't meet.

---

2 Plan for lost time

✔ Look at your chart and see the effects of unpredictable delays and how they can affect the rest of your day or week.

Lost time accumulated over a period creates a surprisingly large impact on the time available for other activities. You get a 'build-up' of negative time. It is always useful to plan pockets of space in your day so that these can be accommodated. In this way, pressure is released and order can be established once again.

TOP TIP
If you use any time management systems, start off simply so that success is assured. You may find you have to manage

---

**expectations better. When asked for
deadlines look for some slack to ensure
that you don't force yourself into missing
deadlines. Sometimes when people are
aware of your timings, they build in
slack as well.**

3 Be prepared to change behavioural habits

✓ Be aware of any patterns that characterise the use of
your time. You may find that you are constantly
overrunning in meetings or that you pick up a lot of
spurious work because you are not assertive enough in
saying 'no' (see Chapter 6, 'Communicating assertively
in the workplace'). All these consume time that you may
not have available.

Dealing with disorganised team members

In order to run an efficient team, every person in the team
needs to know exactly what they are doing and how that
fits into what everybody else is doing.

✓ If a team member is disorganised, you need to get
this person to stand back from what they are doing
and look at the patterns or behaviour they are
exhibiting and the timeline they and the department
are working to. How does this person's contribution
fit in and where are the priorities?

Often time management requires a change in habitual behaviour. This can only be achieved by building awareness, charting a clear route and rewarding success.

Step three: Prioritise and plan ahead

✔ Look at your workload if work is the issue, and categorise your tasks into those that are important to your overall role, those which will add benefit to your role but may not be central and those things that you do that you may be good at but which are outside your area of responsibility.

We often get caught up in responding to others' expectations and sacrificing our own choices. As you undertake your time audit, make sure that you're not spending time on unnecessary activities that do not serve your purpose. Delegate wherever you can but don't expect others to do what you can't do or pick up the mess you leave.

The central point is that planning is essential. Be aware of time pressures. Awareness must always precede action.

Prioritise and plan ahead: Time management toolkits

There are a number of time management toolkits that help people order their days but they are only as useful as the time invested in using them. Many time management courses teach you how to use process to prioritise your task and activities. Remember that your view of what is a priority may be different from another's. So in using these toolkits, you need to build in communication time to ensure that misunderstandings do not occur. Some commercially available toolkits and techniques include:

- BlackBerrys®
- organisers
- 'to do' lists
- categorising work according to its level of importance and focusing only on the essential
- aligning tasks to business goals and objectives and cutting out the 'nice to do'
- shared diaries – team, secretarial, professional groups

Making the transition from using a diary and a bundle of Post-It™ notes to organise your life to using a computerised device such as a BlackBerry® is not easy.

✔ Plan the time it will take to learn the new technology and transfer your information. Only allow a month during which you use a dual system then throw the paper diary away.

New technology can be intimidating, but where there's a will there's a way. You will soon find your new system as convenient as any other you may have used in the past, if not more so.

TOP TIP
Always plan ahead and try to anticipate the pressure of commitments that you make. Make sure that as you plan, you not only build in time for reflecting and learning, but you build in time for yourself.

Common mistakes

✗ **You buy a new gadget that you don't need or want**

In moments of desperation, people often rush out and buy the latest time management technology, which can be both expensive and complicated to use. It is always worth considering what is motivating the purchase – you cannot impose a system when the inclination is not there to use it. Once you have got to the root of the problem and can see what the cause is, you'll be able to identify the most suitable approach to time management.

✗ You expect too much of yourself and become disenchanted

A new environment takes some getting used to. So when we try to change too many things at once, pressure is bound to cause us to step back into habit. While the logic in time management appears straightforward, the complexity of our lives means that managing time is not straightforward. The answer is to take small steps, heading toward clear goals.

✗ You're not prepared to break bad habits and don't ask for help from family and colleagues

How we manage our time can become habitual. You know those people that are always late or those people that are always early. The way you plan your life and time rapidly takes on a pattern. Breaking that pattern can mean that we have to change the way we view ourselves, view the world in which we live and ask for help and support from others in making that change.

STEPS TO SUCCESS

✔ Time management is about making the *most effective* use of your time, both at home and at work.

✔ Awareness is all. Being aware of how you apportion your time, and how those around you spend theirs, is essential for good time management.

✔ A good place to start is to conduct a 'time audit' (as
described above), which will help to make you more
aware of the balance between your work life and
personal life, and between the different jobs you do while
at work.

✔ Remember that there are always choices to be made –
and be prepared to make them. Change the habits of a
lifetime!

✔ You cannot plan your time down to the last minute. Be
honest about the amount of time tasks are likely to take,
and allow pockets of time for unexpected delays.

✔ Don't try to make all the changes at once – you will be
far more likely to slip back into your old habits. Build
them up over a period of time and you will soon see the
difference.

Useful links

Mindtools.com:
www.mindtools.com/pages/main/newMN_HTE.htm
Time Management training programmes:
www.tsuccess.dircon.co.uk/timemanagementtips.htm
ISYS Time Limited:
www.isys-group.co.uk/_page/index2.htm

Avoiding information overload

Thanks to new technology, communication demands and instant data access, the amount of information available to us is rapidly increasing.

The problem is that we have had to absorb all this without any preparation or training. Many people find it stressful and feel themselves slowly sinking in a sea of data.

The scale of the problem

Although information overload is a fairly recent phenomenon, it is already causing casualties. Managers often feel that they have to keep up with the information flow in order to perform well, yet increasing amounts of time are required to enable them to get through the massive amounts of data available. This is resulting in stress and, in some cases, burnout. A worldwide survey conducted by Reuters found that two thirds of managers suffer from increased tension and one third from ill health because of information overload. Some of the symptoms of stress – such as a reduction in decision-making capabilities, short-term memory problems and an inability to concentrate – only exacerbate information overload pressure.

There are, however, ways you can reduce the burden.

Step one: Take control of the problem

Information management, like time management, is a matter of discipline. You need to set boundaries around how much time you're prepared to spend processing information.

✔ Decide what your limits are and create a personal information management system that works for you. This may be setting boundaries around the time you spend responding to e-mails, filtering them through your assistant (if you're lucky enough to have one) or responding only to those e-mails that hold high importance for you.

TOP TIP
Draw up some criteria that determine what you allow through your filter and what you exclude. This may mean putting priorities on your e-mails and deleting those that are low priority, returning calls only to those people you need to speak to, and only looking at a piece of data once before deciding what to do with it. If you miss something important, you can be sure that it will come back to you.

✔ Identify any time-wasting information and eliminate it. Ask to be removed from the list of often unnecessary 'all staff' e-mails; request a good spam filter from the IT department; ask for a summary of overly long minutes or reports.

Step two: Seek information efficiently

✓ Aim for the 'Pareto principle' when seeking information. In other words, 20 per cent of what has been accessed probably holds 80 per cent of the information you need. It's anxiety that propels people to spend excessive time wading through every piece of data available. People used to make decisions in ambiguous situations; it was considered to be a management skill. Aim for developing your instincts along with your knowledge.

✓ Find your own preferred places for accessing information and discipline yourself to go there only. Failing this, you could make use of the information officers in the library of your professional body. They are experienced at finding relevant information and can often save you a great deal of time.

✓ Resist temptation. Only look at data that is relevant to your job, the project you are working on or the decision you are making. Resist the temptation to be intrigued by those things that lie outside your area of responsibility. Too often, people are sucked in to irrelevant detail because they don't know where to draw the line.

✓ Set yourself a time limit. If you haven't found the information you need within the specified time, ask for support, delegate or where possible, try to manage without that information.

TOP TIP

The advantage and disadvantage of the Web is that it's freely available – anyone can set up a website, whether it's poor quality or not, and you can spend hours getting lost in useless websites while looking for the high-quality information you need. Being very specific in your searches will eliminate some of the time that you spend looking for the kind of information you want, as will adding the most productive sites to your list of favourites. Otherwise, you may want to set time boundaries around your Web searches, knowing that you will probably pick up most of the information you need in the first ten minutes or so.

Step three: Learn to say 'no'

✔ Try not to be the dumping ground for information that others don't want to go through. Many will try to pass the burden on to you if you even hint at being receptive to the task. Take control of what passes over your desk and decide not to be held to ransom by a piece of data.

✔ Limit your availability. Leave your mobile phone switched off for periods during the day when you can be quiet and restful or let your voicemail field calls for you. This way you can determine who to speak to and when to schedule the conversations. Anyone who has an urgent need will find a way of getting through to you.

Step four: Manage information

✔ Learn to throw things away. Have the courage to throw data away or delete files when you have exhausted their usefulness. You can always access the same data again and, probably when you do, it will have been updated.

✔ Use the principles of time management. Organising your time effectively may well help with information overload. Surfing the Web is incredibly seductive, with each link taking you further and further into fascinating but unnecessary detail. Decide how much time you'll spend in each session, print the information that is relevant and leave the rest in the ether. You often pick up all the information you need in a few hits, the remainder being less fruitful.

TOP TIP
It may seem rather self-defeating to resort to technology to solve a problem that technology produced in the first place, but there are useful electronic devices such as the iPhone or BlackBerry® that can help alleviate information overload. They have many functions that can be accessed while travelling: you can read your e-mails, edit

**documents, plan meetings, write reports and
even read the newspaper. Any changes will be
automatically transferred to your PC when
you get back to the office.**

Common mistakes

✗ You get bogged down in detail

Getting drawn into the detail of all the information that's
available wastes a lot of time and creates undue stress.
People often fear they'll miss an essential piece of
information if they don't comb through every available
source. In fact this rarely happens. Resist the temptation
to go through every detail that appears on your screen or
comes over your desk.

✗ You fail to prioritise

Being able to prioritise information will make it more
manageable. You may even find that you can delegate
some of the processing to a member of your team,
outlining what they should focus on and report back to
you.

✗ You never switch off

Not being able to switch off from the need to absorb or
generate information can induce a serious stress
reaction. Blood pressure can rise, mental faculties can
deteriorate and any patience you may have had can
disappear altogether. Just as the body needs time to

relax, so does the mind – and not just when it's in the sleep state. Quieting the mind through techniques such as meditation or yoga has been proven to increase health, improve memory and stimulate creativity. It has also been linked to increased productivity and a sense of well-being. If these techniques don't appeal, try other recuperative pursuits such as listening to music, reading, or taking gentle exercise. Anything that allows the mind to 'freewheel' will prove beneficial.

STEPS TO SUCCESS

✔ People often feel that in order to perform well they have to spend more and more time going through the huge amount of information being passed around electronically.

✔ Developing a personal information management system will help you keep on top of the flood of information.

✔ It is important to be selective in the sources you use. Don't be drawn into the web of irrelevant information on the Internet – choose your Favourites, then use them!

✔ Employ technology to control the flow of information – divert e-mails, use voicemail and be prepared to switch your mobile phone off to prevent interruptions.

✔ Remember to throw away (and recycle) printouts and

delete files and e-mails when you have finished with them. There is no need to hoard information – if it is important it can always be accessed.

✔ In order to absorb data effectively you must learn to 'switch off' and give your mind the chance to digest the information.

Useful links

Computer Bits—Information Overload:
www.computerbits.com/archive/1998/0200/infoload.html
InfoWorld business resources:
www.infoworld.com
iPhone:
www.apple.com/uk/iphone
BlackBerry®
http://uk.blackberry.com

Thinking around problems

New ways of thinking can help you solve problems and therefore reduce stress. It is estimated that human beings only use 10 per cent of their brain capacity, so clearly we have vast untapped thinking potential. Exercising the brain in a variety of new ways allows us to expand into those unused capacities.

Our thinking styles develop over the years and become habitual – particularly those we form as we pass through the education system, which tend to focus on the skills of analysis. So when people make statements like 'I'm not creative', or 'I'm not really a thinker', all this means is that they haven't been introduced to, or adopted, different ways of using their minds.

Can one process solve every problem?

In most situations, it is a good idea to allow people to understand problems and then solve them in their own way. However, using tried and tested techniques of problem-solving – ones that are plainly mapped out and used uniformly – allows others to understand the problem and the areas being explored. The process ensures that all the people involved have the opportunity to actively participate in solving the problem at any stage.

While problems *are* always different, there are some common approaches and processes for solving them. Problems can be diagnosed and the various elements can be identified – whether you're talking about problems in the postroom, a manufacturing roadblock or an IT systems failure. Obviously, as an organisation grows in size, so too does the need for more sophisticated techniques.

Step one: Identify the problem

Understanding a problem requires an ability to see it in its entirety – in breadth, depth and context. Here are a number of ways to evaluate the scope of a problem:

- **Recognition** – can you see or feel the problem? Is it isolated, or part of a bigger problem?
- **Symptoms** – how is it showing itself?
- **Causes** – why has it happened?
- **Effects** – what else is being affected by it?

The task then is to break the main problem down into smaller problems, in order to determine whether you are the right person or team to handle it. If not, you need to transfer the problem-solving process to those better equipped to deal with it. If you are, you need to ask additional questions, including: Do you have the right resources? How long might the process take? What are some of the obstacles? What is the anticipated benefit? Once you get answers, move on to the next step.

Step two: Gather data

There are two important questions here: What do you need to know, and how are you going to get it? Most information can be accessed, but there are often time and resource issues involved with collecting and analysing it. Remember that data collection may involve investigating the symptoms of the problem, the underlying causes and/or the overall effects of the problem. Each may have different implications as to how the problem is viewed. Data-gathering techniques include:

- workflow analysis;
- surveys and questionnaires;
- flow charts;
- group and/or one-to-one interviews.

Step three: Think systematically

With the mass of information available these days, the following techniques can be useful to determine what is important and how best to make sense of it.

I SWOT analysis

This is used to identify Strengths and Weaknesses and to examine the existing Opportunities and Threats. Answering questions in each of the four areas enables you to think systematically about a problem and potential solutions. Say, for example, your main headache at work was about the launching of a new product in a tricky market. The SWOT analysis could work as follows:

Strengths: What are some advantages of your new product that the public has been seeking? What are the features that distinguish it from rival products?

Weaknesses: Where are the areas of vulnerability or weakness? Is the price a barrier?
What could be improved? Would different product features make it better?
What are the known vulnerabilities in the market? Is the product launch time-sensitive?

Opportunities: Where are the opportunities in terms of technology, markets, policy and social trends?
Have you got a new commercial idea or found a new way of doing things?
Can you capitalise on what rivals did wrong?

Threats: What barriers do you face? Is your target market right?
Are you facing a change in regulations? Should you wait until it is official?
Is the competition stealing a march on you?
Are there threats to your financial situation? Should you try to raise money now, or wait for a better time?

2 Decision trees

Decision trees allow decisions to be made in situations
where there is a great deal of information to sift through.
They create a framework in which you can examine
alternative solutions and their impact.

✔ Start your decision tree on one side of a piece of paper,
with a symbol representing the decision to be made.
Different lines representing various solutions open out
like a fan from this nexus. Additional decisions or
uncertainties that need to be resolved are indicated on
these lines and, in turn, form the new decision point,
from which yet more options fan out.

3 Critical path analysis

This is another way of approaching complex projects. It
allows you to determine when certain activities should be
completed, so that a project may finish on time and on
budget. The essential concept behind it is that some
activities are dependent on others being completed first
(sequential), and others may be completed more or less at
any time (parallel). The ordering of these activities creates the
critical path through the project.

4 Mind maps

Developed by Tony Buzan, these are graphical tools used
to represent whatever is on your mind. They help you get
everything down on paper, with no initial emphasis on

ordering or prioritising. Mind maps can help you to find your way around a complex subject area, enabling you to visualise how the constituent parts are interrelated. They could be a useful first step in seeing how the land lies and identifying throughways.

✔ Start with a circle on a large sheet of paper. Inside the circle put the word or picture that best represents the idea you wish to explore. Then place other words – perhaps in smaller circles – around the hub. Let your mind wander, and bring in a galaxy of associated words and images. Finally, connect the circles with lines, accenting similar themes with colours or symbols. Once everything is down, you can study how the various 'satellites' relate to the hub, and how you want to apply the content to your personal goals.

TOP TIP

You can be an extremely intelligent person and still have difficulty coming up with solutions to problems. This is probably because you're caught up in your habitual mode of thinking. Thinking styles build up over the years, and we maintain them because they work, in most circumstances. However, they can also limit your ability to think in a freeform way. Try some of the techniques listed in this chapter and challenge yourself to break old habits and think in new ways.

Step four: Think creatively

Techniques that extend our thinking into the more creative realms include:

1 Brainstorming

This is a well-known technique for generating options, where every idea submitted is treated positively. This 'anything goes' approach often stimulates the presentation of viable ideas that wouldn't otherwise have been thought of. Word associations and oblique ideas are all welcomed. It is only in the final stages, when all ideas have been collected, that the honing and prioritising process begins.

TOP TIP

In meetings where brainstorming is not part of the agenda, there often isn't time to indulge someone's creative effort, as it can lead proceedings away from the central aim of the meeting. However, the people who veer off into fanciful realms are probably just demonstrating their natural form of thinking, and may get really frustrated when you curtail them. Try explaining what kind of thinking you are looking for in that particular setting, and offer them another context in which they can freewheel helpfully. Many companies have research and development departments that

---

**encourage off-the-wall thinking, for example,
and they manage to bring extraordinarily
innovative products to market.**

2 Questioning

✔ Ask why a problem is occurring, and then ask again –
four more times. This allows you to drill down and get to
the heart of the matter.

✔ Ask the six universal questions to explore the full extent
of a problem: What? Where? When? How? Why? Who?

3 Six thinking hats

This is a powerful technique developed by lateral thinking
pioneer, Edward de Bono.

✔ Allocate each individual – alone or in a group – a series of
imaginary hats, which represent different outlooks,
according to colour. This forces people to move into
different modes of thinking. White hats focus on the
data, look for gaps, extrapolate from history, and
examine future trends. Red hats use intuition and
emotion to look at problems. Black hats look at the
negative, and find reasons why something may not
work. If an idea can get through this process, it is more
likely to succeed. Yellow hats think positively. This hat's
view helps you to see the benefits of a decision. Green
hats develop creative, freewheeling solutions. There is

no room for criticism in this mode; it is strictly positive. Blue hats orchestrate the meeting – you're in control in this hat. Feel free to propose a new hat to keep ideas flowing.

Step five: Weigh up potential solutions

Taking time to identify the most appropriate solution from your range of options is very important. Suggestions need to be winnowed down to a shortlist, containing only the most realistic possibilities.

To do this, set some hard measures.

✔ Try to determine the costs and benefits of the suggested solutions. If, for example, you feel that outside investment is needed to solve a particular problem, work out the payback period. You can then assess whether your senior management team will accept it.

✔ Analyse each potential solution in turn. Force field analysis is a useful technique for this. By being able to look at the forces that will support or challenge a decision (such as finances or market conditions), you are in a position to strengthen the pros and diminish the cons. Draw three columns, and place the situation or issue in the middle. The pros push on one side, and the cons on the other. Allocate scores to each force to show its potency. This allows you to measure the overall advantages and disadvantages of any given action.

The chosen solution needs to meet some key criteria. Do you have the necessary people, money and time to achieve it? Will you get a sufficient return on investment? Is the solution acceptable to others involved in the situation? Draw up:

- a rationale of why you have reached your particular conclusion;
- a set of criteria to judge the solution's success;
- a plan of action and contingencies;
- a schedule for implementation;
- a team to carry out, be responsible for, and approve the solution.

Step six: Put the chosen solution into action

Implementation means having action plans with relevant deadlines and contingencies built in. Any implementation needs constant review, and the implementation team needs to make sure they have the support of relevant management. Keep asking:

- Are deadlines being met?
- Are team members happy, and is communication strong within and from the team?
- Has the team been recognised for their achievements?
- Are the improvements measurable?
- Is the situation reviewed regularly?

Step seven: Measure success

This is where the two most important questions are asked:

- How well did it work?
- What did we learn from the process?

All experience can be valuable in terms of adding in-house knowledge and expertise.

✔ Think of creating a case study that can be shared with others – either at a conference or directly.

✔ Canvass people's opinions regarding the effectiveness of the process and its outcome. Ask for areas of improvement that could be incorporated into a second phase.

✔ Don't be scared of involving your clients in any evaluation; this can convey a positive message if handled properly, and builds trust in your ability to troubleshoot problems and implement solutions.

Common mistakes

✗ **You tackle too large a problem**
Don't take on problems that lie beyond the control of the team. People often tackle problems that are too general – focus on what is specific and achievable.

✗ You assume everyone thinks like you do

To be productive in groups, you need a diverse range of ways of contributing. Look around you at work; you'll probably recognise different thinking styles and recall how those have led to better clarity, decisions and outcomes. Try to get representatives from different parts of the business to give a different angle on the problem.

✗ You are critical of others' creativity

Under pressure, it is easy to think: 'The last thing I need is flaky ideas when I've got a deadline!' But when you're not stressed, you've probably seen the immense value that creativity can bring. Try not to stifle creative thought; rather, guide and control it openly, alternately encouraging and focusing it as needed.

✗ You get too used to a lack of structure

Entrepreneurial businesses are often formed as a result of an extraordinarily creative mind. However, sooner or later, these businesses need structure. Focused thinking and systems thinking will be necessary for good decision-making and management. For a business to grow, the creative thinkers will have to accommodate the practical, analytical thinkers.

✗ You get carried away by the process

Often, when running workshops, the process becomes more important than the ideas and intellectual discussion. Don't try to use too many techniques. Be aware that excessive creativity can often derail a problem-solving process. Getting the balance right between understanding the problem and finding imaginative solutions requires strong facilitation.

STEPS TO SUCCESS

✓ Thinking styles develop over the years and become habitual, so use your untapped mind potential by thinking in different ways.

✓ Analyse the situation and determine what is important by looking at strengths and weaknesses and examining existing opportunities and threats.

✓ Examine alternative solutions by using graphic representations, like decision trees and mind maps, that let you explore your ideas more fully.

✓ Extend your thinking into the more creative realms by brainstorming and fostering different perspectives and points of attack. Question why a problem is occurring and ask more and more questions to get to the heart of the matter.

✓ In a group, let each member take on a different outlook to force new modes of thinking: emotional, positive, negative, creative and factual.

✓ Assess the impact of the solution and identify areas for improvement in your problem-solving processes.

Useful links

Buzan Centres:

www.mind-map.com/index.htm

Edward de Bono's website:

www.edwdebono.com

Innovative thinking resources for entrepreneurs:

www.innovationtools.com

The Learning Partnership:

www.thelearningpartnership.com

The Open Directory Project:

http://dmoz.org/Science/Social_Sciences/Psychology/Creativity

Tony Buzan's website:

www.thinkbuzan.com/uk

5 Delegating tasks

Mastering the skill of delegation will help you manage your time and therefore reduce your stress levels. But it is often when we are most stressed that we delegate least. It is easy to panic and to cut yourself off from your colleagues or employees at times when you need their support the most.

But delegation isn't just about making your workload lighter by giving tasks to others. It is also about getting staff to take full responsibility for certain key functions. In order for a business to grow and for employees to find new paths of development, new people must be employed to take over established functions allowing others to develop different aspects of the business.

Benefits of delegation

Delegation is not an easy option. It does not make things easier (there will always be other challenges), but it does make things more efficient and effective. It is essentially a more interactive way of working with a team of people, involving instruction, training and development. You'll need to invest some time and effort to do it effectively, but the long-term benefits will make it worth your while.

Step one: Know when to delegate

Delegation is fundamental to management, so look for opportunities to do it. These may include:

- when you have too much work to do to complete all your tasks;
- when you don't have enough time to devote to all-important tasks;
- when it is clear that certain staff need to develop, particularly new employees;
- when an employee has the skills needed to perform a specific task.

Step two: Know what to delegate

✔ Delegate the routine administrative tasks that take up too much of your time. There may be small routine things which you've always done, which you may even enjoy doing, but which are an inappropriate use of time.

✔ Delegate projects which it makes sense for one person to handle. These will be a good test of how a person manages and co-ordinates their work. Give the person something they can do, and not impossible tasks at which others have failed – this might be a damaging experience for the person concerned.

✔ Delegate tasks for which an employee has a special aptitude or enthusiasm. Make the most of your team's skills and passions.

✔ Don't get bogged down in relationship management. Liaising with a person or organisation is an important but often time-consuming task. It can be delegated.

Step three: Know whom to delegate to

Staff development is a vital part of delegation. It is therefore very important to have a good understanding of the people you can delegate tasks to. The approach should be adapted according to the individual. They must have the skills and ability or at least the potential to develop into the role and be someone you can trust.

✔ Test your staff out with small tasks to help show you what they can do. Do they show good time management skills? Do they keep a diary? Do they make notes? Training may be given or these skills developed in the person through delegation.

✔ The employee must be available for the assignment, and the people who do effective work should not be overburdened.

✔ Try to delegate tasks out among as many employees as possible, and remember to consider the option of assigning a task to two or more people.

TOP TIP
Responsibilities should not be delegated
without also conferring the authority to
discharge those responsibilities.

Step four: Delegate interactively

✔ Think positive. The manager has the right to delegate and must delegate. It will not happen perfectly first time. Your ability to delegate will improve with experience. Try to act decisively and avoid prevarication – you may need to learn more assertiveness skills. A positive approach will also give the person you're delegating to confidence in themselves. It's important for them to feel that the manager believes in them.

TOP TIP
Be patient and have faith in the people around
you. One of the reasons you are delegating is
to relieve yourself of stress, not to add to your
burden by constantly worrying about the
person doing a good job.

✔ Plan ahead. If you expect the person to be efficient, you'll need to make sure that you yourself are well organised. If there is no overall plan of what is going on, it will be hard to identify, schedule and evaluate the work you've asked others to do. Schedule time to develop and assess the person in the job. Do you have a plan for their development? Are there notes about how they are doing? You'll need to assess the task and then decide how much responsibility the person should be given. Prepare before seeing the person, but don't use this as a pretext for delay.

✓ Discuss the tasks and problems in depth with the person you are delegating to, and explain clearly what is expected of them. It is crucial to give precise objectives, but let them ask questions too. The employee should participate in setting the parameters. They need to understand why they are doing the task, where it fits into the scheme of things. Ask them how they will go about the task, discuss the plan and the support they might need.

✓ Set deadlines and schedule them into diaries. What has been agreed should be summarised and notes taken about what each employee is required to do. If the person is given a lot of creative scope and is being tested out, you may decide to be deliberately vague. If the task is urgent and critical, it will be essential to be specific.

✓ Support your employees. The degree of support you give will depend upon the development of the person, and your relationship with them. In the early stages it can be appropriate to work with the person, to share certain tasks. You'll be able to back off more as your understanding of their abilities increases. Encourage them to come back if they have any problems. While it is important to have time to yourself, you need to be accessible if the person has a problem, or the situation changes. Try not to interfere or criticise if things are going according to plan.

TOP TIP
Focus on results rather than methods. If the person you are delegating to doesn't carry out the task in the way you would have done, don't rush to interfere or criticise. Your way works best for you, but it may not work so well for someone else.

✔ Monitor progress. It is too easy to forget all about the task until the completion date. In the meantime, all sorts of things could have gone wrong. When planning, build in time to review progress. If more problems were expected to arise and nothing has been heard then you may want to check with the employee. Otherwise schedule in routine meetings. Deadlines and objectives may have to be altered as the situation changes.

✔ Review performance. You can discuss career development issues in appraisals, and note the results of delegated tasks for this purpose. When a task is complete remember to give praise and review how it went. If the person has failed to deliver, this should also be discussed. When you're delegating responsibility, it is important to hold people responsible for what they do.

✔ Reward achievement but don't promise rewards if
   they can't be delivered: there may be limits on what
   you can offer. If a person's responsibilities are increased,
   they should receive fair rewards for it. Rewards might
   depend upon the overall success of the business, but
   development can carry its own rewards.

Common mistakes

Stress is one of several reasons why people find it difficult to
delegate. Here are some of the other obstacles, any one of
which might put you off delegating when you are under a lot
of pressure:

✗ **You think that you're saving time**
   It seems quicker to do it yourself than to bother
   explaining the task and correcting mistakes.

✗ **You doubt your employees' ability**
   You cannot overcome a fear that the person will not be
   successful and will create even more problems than they
   solve.

✗ **You worry about your status**
   An employee who is quick on the uptake and does well
   can take over the role of being the person everyone goes
   to with their problems. Maybe you feel threatened by
   their competence. They may even find something wrong
   with the way you do things.

✗ **You lack confidence**
If you find it hard to give instructions, this will be an obstacle, as you'll actively avoid delegation. If problems arise, or if the person fails to discharge their responsibilities, you may doubt your own ability to confront the person about their actions.

✗ **You neglect staff development**
Having given staff increased responsibilities, you may not be confident of being able to reward them sufficiently. Conversely, some people hesitate to delegate tasks that are too tedious.

✗ **You hide ignorance of delegation skills**
While you know that delegation is necessary, you don't know where to start – so you don't.

STEPS TO SUCCESS

✔ Mastering the skill of delegation will mean that everyone benefits – it will help you manage your time and it will aid staff development, improving overall productivity.

✔ Don't let stress get in the way of delegation. When you are under pressure, passing tasks on – to the right person – will save you time in the end.

✔ Remember to delegate interactively – get to know your staff, listen to their worries and discover their strengths.

✔ Successfully passing responsibility down the line is key to company growth.

✔ Remember to delegate assertively. Your confidence will be transferred on to the person you're delegating to.

✔ Don't forget that when you delegate, you remain ultimately responsible for the results of the work you have delegated.

Useful links

businessballs.com:
www.businessballs.com/delegation.htm
Getahead-direct.com:
www.getahead-direct.com/gwtm07-successful-delegation.htm
Jobserve.com:
www.jobserve.com/news/NewsStory.asp?SID=2009
Mindtools.com:
www.mindtools.com/tmdelegt.html

Communicating assertively in the workplace

Do you find that people get the better of you at work, that you're always the one who draws the short straw and ends up doing things that you would rather not do? Does this end up making you resentful or unhappy because you feel unable to confront the situation?

Assertiveness is an approach to communication that honours your choices as well as those of the person you are communicating with. It is not about being aggressive and steamrollering your colleague into submission. Rather, it is about seeking and exchanging opinions, developing a full understanding of the issues and negotiating a win-win situation.

Ask yourself these questions to determine your level of assertiveness:

- Do you feel 'put upon' or ignored in your exchanges with colleagues?
- Are you unable to speak your mind and ask for what you want?
- Do you find it difficult to stand up for yourself in a discussion?
- Are you inordinately grateful when

someone seeks your opinion and takes it into account?

If you answer 'yes' to most of these questions, you may need to consider becoming more assertive.

Step one: Choose the right approach

Becoming assertive is all about making choices that meet your needs and the needs of the situation. Sometimes it is appropriate to be passive – if you were facing a snarling dog, you might not want to provoke an attack by looking for a win-win situation! There may be other occasions, however, when aggression is the answer. However, this is still assertive behaviour as *you*, rather than other people or situations, are in control of how you react.

TOP TIP
After a lifetime of being the way they are, some people are daunted by the prospect of change. But if you don't change what you do, you'll never change what you get. All it takes to change is a decision. Once you have made that decision, you will naturally observe yourself in situations, notice what you do and don't do well and then you can try out new behaviours to see what works for you.

✔ You may find it helpful to investigate some specially tailored training courses so that you can try out some approaches before taking on a colleague or manager in a 'live' situation. This sort of thing takes practice.

Step two: Practise projecting a positive image

✔ Use 'winning' language. Rather than saying 'I always come off worst!' say 'I've learned a great deal from doing lots of different things in my career. I'm now ready to move on'. This is the beginning of taking control in your life.

✔ Visualise what you wish to become, make the image as real as possible, and feel the sensation of being in control. Perhaps there have been moments in your life when you naturally felt like this, a time when you have excelled. Recapture that moment and 'live' it again. Imagine how it would be if you felt like that in other areas of your life. Determine to make this your goal and recall this powerful image or feeling when you are getting disheartened. It will re-energise you and keep you on track.

TOP TIP
If you are small in stature, it's easy to think
you can't have presence because people will
overlook you. But many of the most

**successful people, in business and in
entertainment, are physically quite small.
Adopting an assertive communication style
and body language has the effect of making
you look more imposing. Assume you have
impact, visualise it, feel it, breathe it.**

Step three: Condition others to take you seriously

This can be done through non-verbal as well as verbal communication.

✔ If someone is talking over you and you are finding it difficult to get a word in edgeways, you can hold up your hand signalling 'stop' as you begin to speak. 'I hear what you are saying but I would like to put forward an alternative viewpoint . . . '

✔ Always take responsibility for your communication. Use the 'I' word. 'I would like . . . ', 'I don't agree . . . ', 'I am uncomfortable with this . . . '

✔ Being aware of non-verbal communication signals can also help you build rapport. If you mirror what others are doing when they are communicating with you, it will help you get a sense of where they are coming from and how to respond in the most helpful way.

TOP TIP
Until you get used to being assertive, you may
find it hard to say 'no' to people. One useful
technique is to say, 'I'd like to think about this
first. I'll get back to you shortly'. Giving
yourself time and space to rehearse your
response can be really helpful.

Step four: Use positive body language

✔ Stand tall, breathe deeply and look people in the eye
when you speak to them.

✔ Instead of anticipating the negative outcome, expect
something positive.

✔ Listen actively to the other party and try putting yourself
in their shoes so that you have a better chance of
seeking the solution that works for you both.

✔ Enquire about their thoughts and feelings by using
'open' questions, that allow them to give you a full
response rather than just 'yes' or 'no'. Examples include:
'Tell me more about why . . . ', 'How do you see this
working out?', and so forth.

✔ Don't let people talk down to you when you're sitting
down. If they're standing, stand up too!

61

Step five: Recognise different communication styles

There are four types of communication style:

- **aggressive** – where you win and everyone else loses
- **passive** – where you lose and everyone else wins
- **passive/aggressive** – where you lose and do everything you can (without being too obvious) to make others lose too
- **assertive** – where everyone wins

It's important to appreciate that people communicate in a variety of ways. Your assertiveness therefore needs to be sensitive to a range of possible responses. Here are some tips on how to deal with the different communication styles outlined above:

✔ **Passive/aggressive people.** If you are dealing with someone behaving in a passive/aggressive manner, you can handle it by exposing what he or she is doing. 'I get the feeling you are not happy about this decision' or 'It appears you have something to say on this; would you like to share your views now?' In this way, they either have to deny their passive/aggressive stance or they have to disclose their motivations. Either way, you are left in the driving seat.

✔ **Passive people.** If you are dealing with a passive person, rather than let them be silent, encourage them to contribute so that they can't put the blame for their disquiet on someone else.

✔ **Aggressive people.** The aggressive communicator may need confronting but do it carefully; you don't want things to escalate out of control. Using the 'I'd like to think about it first' technique is often useful in this instance. The main thing to remember is that you have equal rights to everyone else, equal rights to be taken into account, and to say 'no'. Remember this when you are feeling badgered or defeated by someone.

Conflict is notorious for bringing out the aggression in people. However, it is still possible to be assertive in this context. You may need to show that you are taking them seriously by reflecting their energy. To do this, you could raise your voice to match the volume of theirs, then bring the volume down as you start to explore what would lead to a win-win solution. 'I CAN SEE THAT YOU ARE UPSET and I would feel exactly the same if I were you . . . However . . . ' Then you can establish the desired outcome for both of you.

If you become more assertive, people won't necessarily think that you have become more aggressive. Be responsive to their communication styles, and their needs will be met too. All that will happen is that your communication style becomes more effective.

TOP TIP

Once you become assertive, your confidence
level will be boosted, yet you need to have
sufficient levels of confidence to try it in the
first place. If you feel you lack the confidence
to confront people, try the technique out in a
safe environment first so that you get used to
how it feels, then you can start to use it more
widely.

Common mistakes

✗ You go too far at first

Many people, when trying out assertive behaviour for the
first time, find that they go too far and become
aggressive. Remember that you are looking for a win-
win, not a you-win-and-they-lose situation. Take your
time. Observe yourself in action. Practise and ask for
feedback from trusted friends or colleagues.

✗ Others react negatively to your assertiveness

Your familiar circle of friends will be used to you the way
you were, not the way you want to become. They may try
and make things difficult for you. With your new assertive
behaviour, this won't be possible unless you choose it. If
you find you are in this situation, explain what you are
trying to do and ask for their support. If they are not
prepared to help you, you may wish to choose to let
them go from your circle of friends.

STEPS TO SUCCESS

✔ Try to avoid feeling resentful – if you are feeling 'put upon', act on it!

✔ Remember that sometimes passivity is the best approach. Don't mistake aggressiveness for assertiveness!

✔ Speaking positively and using positive body language will encourage others to take you seriously.

✔ It is important to listen carefully to other people's opinions so you are clear about which points you differ on, and upon which points you agree.

✔ Try your techniques out in a safe environment until you feel comfortable with them.

✔ Build up a toolkit of techniques and responses that have worked for you in the past and reuse them.

Useful links

Assertiveness.com:
www.assertiveness.com
Business Link:
www.businesslink.gov.uk/bdotg/action/layer?site=181&topicId=5000689983
The Oak Tree Counseling Self-Help Assertiveness Quiz:
www.theoaktree.com/assrtquz.htm

Tackling poor morale

Poor morale undermines the commitment of employees, hurts the product or service they offer and can alienate the clients and customers that they serve. It can arise for many reasons – perhaps a difficult economic climate, a clash of cultures after a merger or acquisition or poor management – all of which may result in a high-stress environment.

Poor morale can be so encompassing that, after a while, it is difficult to know how to find its source, and thus how to reverse it. What starts, perhaps, as individual apathy can deteriorate into a generalised problem, and an infectious one at that: it can start in one area and spread to the entire business.

In spite of the insidiousness of poor morale, it *is* reversible. Some ways of doing this are discussed below.

Step one: Consult your employees

✔ If your business is suffering from poor morale and you are unsure why, start by asking your employees. Many organisations conduct regular surveys to assess the feelings and opinions of the workforce. Try to understand what tools or resources people need to make their work, and work environment, more satisfying. It is important to identify people's expectations, their wages and benefits, how the internal communication system is working and whether the management style is too cumbersome, oppressive or bureaucratic. You might also explore areas such as reward and recognition, and seek tangible ways for people to contribute to the process of change.

Step two: Manage an organisational survey properly

Organisational surveys tend to elicit comments on the way a business is run, and therefore give senior management lots to think about. The act of conducting a survey also tends to raise expectations, so unless the business is prepared to address the findings, it is best not to start down this route.

There are several options for conducting an organisational survey. It can be set up internally, an external consultant can be asked to advise on the questions and format or it can be outsourced entirely. Outsourcing can be particularly effective because you gain an independent view that is not coloured by the dominant culture inside the business. It is often difficult to see an organisational trait or judge its impact when you are part of it.

✔ Make sure the survey is conducted confidentially so people can give you honest feedback without fear of repercussions. You may get some extreme comments or jokes, but these can be stripped out in the analysis so that common themes emerge.

✔ Publish the results once the survey has been completed. People will want to see whether their comments have been heeded and what the organisation intends to do about them.

It is not the survey itself that raises morale, but the resulting actions that count. All too often, organisations initiate surveys, but when they find the feedback challenging, they sweep the results aside and hope that the contributors haven't noticed. This is more damaging than not doing anything in the first place.

TOP TIP
Organisational surveys often result in a management team receiving a lot of criticism. People seem to take the opportunity to unleash their grievances, and the whole exercise can become very ugly and political, particularly if they are conducted in a setting where morale is low. It is important that the senior management team is seen to take this seriously, and gives a signal of their intention to do something about the feedback. They will need to promote their response in the company newsletter or magazine, on the

---

intranet or through a series of meetings. They will also need to address some of the specific complaints right away to reassure people that they are listening.

When you are at the centre of a morale problem

Personal problems – a death in the family, for example – and work stress, such as a bad performance review, will affect a team at all levels, including the manager. So how do you get yourself back on track when your morale is the worst in your team? Three of the most effective ways are to:

✓ take a holiday;
✓ share your concerns with a trusted colleague;
✓ undergo professional counselling.

We all need to vent our frustration and anger sometimes, or receive reassurance that we are appreciated. Don't let paths of communication break down when you are feeling low. Consider the following two options:

✓ Explain your circumstances to another senior manager, perhaps using a third party as a facilitator, in order to build new understanding and make a fresh start.
✓ Explain your morale problem to your team, but take a positive approach and tell them your plan for getting back on track, asking for their help.

Communicating in these ways will show that you are
taking charge of your behaviour, and also that you care
about them and value their support.

Step three: Draw up a timetable for change

✔ When setting out a programme of change, put a
timescale behind the actions or initiatives. Some will take
much longer than others, especially if you have
highlighted a need for a full-scale organisational change
initiative. However, there are bound to be some quick
wins identified, which should be implemented straight
away.

✔ Any changes should be publicised, and feedback should
be sought to ensure that they met people's
expectations. These early signs that the organisation is
prepared to take some action will serve as the first boost
to morale, and win greater co-operation with future
initiatives.

Step four: Create a structure

Interestingly, poor motivation often occurs as a result of a
lack of organisational structure or discipline. People need a

framework so that they know where they are in the wider scheme of things. It provides them with a route for getting decisions made or making special requests. This framework should not be inflexible, but it should provide the means by which people can contribute to the success of the business.

✔ Map out and publicise a clear office structure. As morale is improved, the need for structure and discipline diminishes. However, it is important not to let it disappear altogether. You need to strike a good balance between structure and fluidity in all aspects of the business.

TOP TIP

If a senior manager is destroying the good morale of your team by bullying and badgering people whenever she or he comes round, you can ask for a meeting with this person to explain the effects this behaviour has on you and your team. Perhaps he or she has not received feedback on this problem before and may be willing to try a different approach. You could also ask that, when there is something to be said to your team, the manager either allows you to deliver the message yourself, or allows you to facilitate a meeting with the team. In this way, you will be able to get closer to the source of the problem and influence the outcome.

Step five: Get to know your team

On a local level, managers can do much to improve morale. Good managers get to know the people who report to them. This means:

✔ making yourself available when they need to talk or share a problem;

✔ valuing them for their particular skills, passions, and knowledge;

✔ helping them to develop their potential and supporting them in their ambitions.

All too often, managers have a tendency to think of their roles in terms of strategic objectives. They forget that people are the company's most valuable resource, and not merely cogs in a wheel.

By creating a culture of open, constructive feedback, people will feel inclined to co-operate with you as you drive your part of the business forward. Once you start valuing them properly, they will grow in confidence, and their commitment and morale will be raised.

A positive environment with a no-blame culture and lots of praise when things go well is a very satisfying place to work. It is up to managers to play their part in creating such an environment for their teams.

TOP TIP
A company party can be an effective way to raise morale, but it depends greatly on how it is done. If it is simply a sop to keep people quiet for a while, then the shallowness of it will just perpetuate poor morale. However, if it is put in the context of a cultural change, and plans have been put in place to follow through, then it could be a positive way of heralding change.

Common mistakes

✗ **You forget your employees are human**
In the pressured organisational setting, it is easy to forget that people bring their vulnerabilities and aspirations with them to work each day. They don't appreciate being thought of as machines; they respond to human understanding and connection. Managers who enjoy the people side of their job, and who believe there is a way to reach everyone, seldom have trouble with getting the co-operation of their team or building morale.

✗ **You don't acknowledge there is a problem**
Trying to cover up poor morale by denying its existence will only make things worse. It is better to take some sort of action than no action at all – whether in the form of an organisational survey, a company-wide meeting or a

series of focus groups that aim to get to the bottom of the problem. Although it may not be easy to reverse, the source of poor morale is usually plain to see after one of these initiatives has been followed through.

✗ You don't keep up the good work

Tackling poor morale is not a once-in-a-lifetime activity; it needs to be sustained over a period of time. Although this does not ensure that poor morale will not re-emerge, at least it can act as an early warning system. By repeating morale-measuring activities, it is possible to adjust the course of action if things are beginning to slip again. Some companies run yearly organisational surveys to ensure that they are in touch with the opinions of their employees.

STEPS TO SUCCESS

✔ Poor morale can affect commitment, which may in turn alienate colleagues, clients or customers.

✔ If you are having personal problems, take a positive step by having a holiday, seeing a professional counsellor or talking to a trusted colleague.

✔ A manager can reverse poor morale by talking to his/her employees and listening to their opinions, thus creating a culture of open, constructive feedback.

✔ A survey is a good way to get honest answers

confidentially. Outsourcing the survey will lead to a more
objective view of your organisation.

✔ When you have determined the issues affecting morale,
draw up a timescale plan for change and publicise this –
it is important to act on the results so that employees
know their opinions are being taken seriously.

✔ Value your colleagues' individual skills and knowledge
and help them to develop their potential.

Useful links

CIO.com:

www.cio.com/archive/050102/morale.html

Entrepreneur.com

entrepreneur.com

Microsoft bCentral:

www.bcentral.com/articles/krotz/111.asp

About.com:

http://humanresources.about.com/cs/conflictres/a/
negativitycures.htm

BNET:

www.bnet.com/2410-13056_23-63072.html

Dealing with stressful relationships and bullying

One of the most common causes of stress in the workplace is a difficult or challenging relationship with a work colleague – particularly when it is the boss. It can be tempting to lay the blame for this type of situation at the other person's feet, due to his or her unreasonable, negative, awkward or unhelpful behaviour. Whether justified or not in blaming the other person, the good news is that there is still plenty that you can do to change the dynamics of the relationship.

Bullying and physical abuse lie at the extreme end of behaviour, with more subtle and common forms of harassment at the other end. What is tolerated in the workplace will depend very much upon the culture of the organisation and the attitudes and awareness of its leaders. Some businesses ignore all forms of harassment; others make a point of creating a culture where intimidation of any sort is cause for reprimand or dismissal.

It is worth reflecting on your organisation's culture to see what maltreatment exists, both on and under the surface.

Step one: Understand the forms bullying can take

The recipient of bullying is often in a weaker position, physically, emotionally or hierarchically. Victims are usually unable or unwilling to stand up for themselves, due to what they feel will be the unacceptable consequences, such as an escalation of abusive behaviour or the threat of redundancy. This fear allows the behaviour to continue.

Any form of harassment can have a serious impact on the morale of staff in the business, and can affect the performance and health of individuals. Not only is it simply wrong, but it is unlawful, and should be treated seriously.

Harassment can include:

- all manner of physical contact from touching, pushing and shoving, to serious assault;
- intrusive or obsessive behaviours, such as constant pestering, baiting or dogging a person's movements;
- tricks being played that result in risk or danger to the individual;
- group bullying, where the individual is overpowered by a number of aggressors.

Less direct harassment may include:

- the spreading of rumours about the individual, making jokes or offensive personal remarks;

- written statements, letters or graffiti;
- actions that isolate the individual and prevent them from doing their work effectively;
- non co-operation, or sabotage of professional objectives;
- pressure for sexual favours;
- obscene gestures and comments;
- the orchestration of situations that compromise the individual;
- manipulative 'political' behaviours, that may include bribery or blackmail.

TOP TIP
The difference between a good joke and bullying can be subtle. However, if the person being bullied is demeaned and disempowered in some way, or if the joke becomes personally critical and destructive, then the line has been crossed.

Step two: Recognise the mental and physical impact

If you are being bullied, don't be tempted to live with the difficulties of having a troublesome boss or work colleague, seeking ways to minimise the impact he or she has on your working life. Avoidance tactics can be time-consuming and stressful.

✔ Focus on your own well-being as this may encourage you to tackle the issue rationally and try to reach an accommodation that will prevent you from jeopardising your health or feeling that you have to leave your job.

Step three: Determine when the line has been crossed

Often, people find it hard to know whether the line of harassment has been crossed. If they confront the perpetrators, they can be accused of 'being a poor sport', or worse. Such accusations are often levelled to mask what is going on, and can seriously undermine the victim's confidence.

✔ Seek feedback from those who may have observed any incidents. Their account may give you more ammunition to deal with the problem appropriately. Select your witness carefully though – ones you can trust to be allies throughout the ordeal, who won't 'flip' on you under pressure.

Determining whether the harassment is trivial or serious is paramount. If it is infrequent and seems harmless or inadvertent, try not to take it too personally. Remember that bullying says more about the character of the bully than it does about you. However, if the bullying is persistent or escalates, you must confront it and report it.

TOP TIP

If you feel you're being bullied, but the perpetrator disguises his or her actions in jest, one way of dealing with this is to write down the incidents in a journal, including the context in which they took place. Ask for feedback from observers and include their comments. Over time, you will be able to see if there is a pattern to the treatment you have been receiving. Also, the record may be useful if you decide to take the matter further.

✔ Check in the employees' handbook if you have one. There are probably procedures in place to assist you in dealing with your situation. You may be advised to report the incident(s) to your manager but, should you feel uncomfortable about this – for example, if your manager is part of the problem (see below) – you may wish to go directly to the human resources department.

Step four: Dealing with a difficult boss

Many people have a challenging relationship with their boss. When examining such a relationship, it's important to realise how much of it is due to the structure of the organisation – your boss necessarily has to give you tasks, some of which you may not enjoy – and how much is due to truly unreasonable behaviour. Looking at the wider issues in the organisation may provide the key to the problem.

I Understand your boss

'Difficult boss syndrome' is rarely caused simply by a personality clash.

✔ However uncomfortable it may feel, try putting yourself in your boss's shoes. Recognise the objectives that define his or her role and think through the pressures they are under. Make a mental list of your boss's strengths, preferred working style, idiosyncrasies, values and beliefs.

This will help you deepen your understanding. Very often, when we feel disliked or when we dislike someone, we avoid building this understanding and instead look for ways of avoiding the issues.

TOP TIP

If your boss is making work intolerable because of his or her moody and bad-tempered behaviour, try to work out how you could influence the situation for the better. Observe his or her behaviour to see if there is a pattern in it, and then try giving constructive feedback, letting your boss know how his or her mood swings affect you. Use assertive language and ask if there is anything you can do to alleviate the cause of the problem. If the behaviour persists, you may wish to consult your human resources department to see if there are any formal procedures in place to deal with such a situation.

2 Compare the way you both perceive your role

You may feel that you are performing well, but if you are putting your energy into tasks that your boss does not feel are relevant, you will be seen as performing poorly.

✔ Take the initiative to explore your boss's expectations and agree on your objectives. This will clarify your role and give you a better idea of how to progress in the organisation.

TOP TIP
A lack of communication often contributes to workplace misunderstandings. If you feel like you are missing out on opportunities or being denied information because you are not one of your boss's favourites, try approaching him or her for a consultation on your methods and goals. If your boss persists in denying you the information you need, you may have a case of bullying against him or her.

---

3 Ask for the support you need

When managers neglect to give their employees the information and support they need, this creates ambiguity and forces employees to second-guess their boss's requirements.

✓ Ask for the information and resources you need, or find other ways to access these, as this will put you in control of the situation and protect you from the need to improvise.

4 Understand yourself

We very often have poor self-knowledge and are sometimes surprised by our reactions and the feedback we get. In getting to know yourself better, you may wish to ask for input from your colleagues.

✓ Ask your colleagues what they observe when you interact with your boss, how you come across to them and how you could manage your communication differently. Although their perception may not represent the absolute truth about you, it nonetheless reflects the image you create.

5 Consider changing aspects of your behaviour

This often prompts a reciprocal behavioural change in your boss. If you don't change anything about the way you interact with your boss, the relationship will remain unaltered, so this is definitely worth a try.

✓ Think through some of the past encounters you have had with your boss and reflect upon them objectively. Perhaps this situation happens over and over again, which suggests that you harbour a value that is being repeatedly compromised. If you can understand what this is, you can learn to manage these situations effectively.

Perhaps you value attention to detail, but your boss is a big-picture person. Every time you ask for more detailed information, you will draw attention to your boss's vulnerability, and he or she is likely to become uncooperative or irritated by your request. Once you have observed your respective patterns, you can work around them.

6 Remember that a relationship is mutual

In order to be considered effective, managers need a co-operative and productive team. But in order to be part of such a team, each member needs their manager to provide the resources and support they need to do their job properly. It is well known that some of the most stressful situations arise when dependents' needs are not met.

✔ If your boss is making you miserable by constantly making negative comments about your work, suggest that he or she gives you clear guidelines and constructive feedback to help you meet his or her expectations and develop your talents.

Remember that if you are no longer willing to spend time managing your difficult boss, you still have the ultimate power: you can just walk away.

Common mistakes

✗ You mistake a genuine extrovert for a bully

Extroverts frequently speak their minds before really
thinking about what they are saying – which can sound
confrontational and be mistaken for harassment. Being
extroverts, however, they are often receptive to
questioning and keen to point out that they were just
testing the boundaries, or joking. By sharing your
perception and inviting theirs, it is possible to clarify and
dispel the situation without further entanglement.

✗ You take your boss's behaviour personally

It is very tempting to take the behaviour of a difficult boss
personally. However, it is very unlikely that *you* are the
problem. It may be something you do, it may be the
values you hold, or it may be that you remind your boss
of someone he or she doesn't get on with.

✗ You don't remain detached

Many difficult relationships deteriorate to the point where
they are fraught with contempt and confrontation. This is
never helpful in a work setting and only makes matters
uncomfortable for everyone. If you find yourself being
drawn into an angry exchange, try to remain emotionally
detached and listen actively to what is being said (or
shouted) to you. It may provide you with clues about why
the situation has developed and allow you to get straight
to the point of concern. Ask for a private review
afterwards to explore the incident. This may bring to the

surface issues that are relatively easy to deal with and that will prevent further outbursts from occurring.

✗ **You never confront the issue**

Because facing up to harassment is so difficult, many people avoid biting the bullet. Inactivity will only prolong a miserable situation. Acquiescence enables bullying to thrive and allows the aggressors to hold power. Try taking responsibility for your share of the problem and examine what it is you are doing to provoke conflict between you and your boss or colleague.

Useful links

Acas:
www.acas.org.uk
Bully online:
www.bullyonline.org/workbully/index.htm
Bullying and harassment at work:
www.acas.org.uk/publications/AL04.html and
www.acas.org.uk/publications/AL05.html
Dealing with difficult people:
www.ivillage.com/topics/work/0,,416656,00.html
Improve Now.com:
www.improvenow.com
UNISON – advice on work problems:
www.troubleatwork.org.uk/about.asp
Workplace bullying site:
www.workplacebullying.co.uk/links.html
National Bullying Helpline:
www.nationalbullyinghelpline.co.uk

Where to find more help

Don't Sweat the Small Stuff at Work: Simple Ways to Minimize Stress and Conflict While Bringing Out the Best in Yourself and Others
Richard Carlson
London: Hodder Mobius, 1999
284pp ISBN: 0340748737
This is a best-selling, comprehensive guide to combatting stress in your life at work. The book is full of useful advice for dealing with a range of panic-inducing situations, including asking for a pay-rise, coping with presentations and meetings, reacting to a colleague's criticism and handling a difficult boss.

Getting Things Done: The Art of Stress-free Productivity
David Allen
London: Penguin, 2003
267pp ISBN: 978–0142000281
Based on the notion that productivity is proportional to your ability to handle projects in a relaxed manner, the author offers solutions to self-management that minimise stress and enhance one's focus and efficiency.

Time Management from the Inside Out
Julie Morgenstern
London: Hodder & Stoughton, 2001
239pp ISBN: 0340771380
This is a thorough, accessible guide to creating a time management system that works for you and your personal situation. The author sets out to give sound advice that can be customised across a range of lifestyles.

Instant Stress Management
Brian Clegg
London: Kogan Page, 2000
128pp ISBN: 0749431164
This book offers quick, easy-to-use exercises to help individuals to reduce their stress. In addition, three introductory sections discuss stress—where it comes from, medical aspects of stress, and controlling stress—and a brief exercise section focuses on assessment. A final section give further reading and examples of relaxational music.

Managing Employee Stress
Lesley Towner
London: Kogan Page, 1997
128pp ISBN: 0749425261
This is a practical text aiming to teach managers how to recognise and react effectively to signs of employee stress. Chapters cover employers' legal responsibilities; causes, symptoms, and effects of stress; the manager's role; communicating effectively; and preventing or reducing stress at work. A workplace stress inventory, case studies, and self-help stress management measures are included.

The One-minute Meditator: Relieving Stress and Finding Meaning in Everyday Life
Bill Birchard, David A. Nichol
Cambridge, Massachusetts: Perseus, 2001
164pp ISBN: 0738203785
This is a guide to why and how to meditate in short periods of time—in any place and at any time of day. Instead of relieving stress through temporary distractions, the book teaches readers how to quiet their thoughts from within, reaping considerable physical and emotional benefits.